MAD for MATH

EQUISAURS AND PTERO-MEASUREMENTS

EDITED BY

fosforo:

WS Kids
WHITE STAR KIDS

ILLUSTRATIONS BY
AGNESE BARUZZI

TO START WITH...
WELCOME TO "SAURUS" MEASUREMENTS!

"You can know the name of a bird in all the languages of the world, but when you're finished, you'll know absolutely nothing whatever about the bird...So, let's look at the bird and see what it's doing—that's what counts. I learned very early the difference between knowing the name of something and knowing something."
—Richard Feynman

Measuring is an important skill for humans to have. It is a useful and extremely practical action, and it is present in our daily lives. But unless we have a standard of reference for measuring something and can look at it in a wider context, we won't learn very much by just taking a measurement. In this book we want to show you measurements and quantities and how knowing how to look at everything from the right perspective—as always happens in science, but also in our own lives—is a really important skill.

CONTENTS:
In the pages of this book you will find challenges and games with numbers, measurements, and equivalences that have been created to help you exercise and train your problem-solving and observation skills and...
to have fun!

FOR CHILDREN
GRADE 2-3.

A FEW TIPS FOR ADULTS

ALLOW YOUR CHILDREN TO WORK AT THEIR OWN PACE, AND RESPECT THEIR "REFUSALS"!

If they close the book or skip a page, it doesn't necessarily mean they're giving up. They may just need a little time to think about how to solve the problem.

ASK QUESTIONS RATHER THAN GIVE ANSWERS!

If your child asks you for help, don't give them the answer; instead, help them focus on the problem, or their mistake, by asking targeted questions. Let your child find their own way to solve the problem, even if it is long and convoluted. You can then help them explore other, perhaps more "clever," ways to find the solution.

UNDERSTANDING IS THE FIRST STEP TO PROBLEM-SOLVING

Help your child work through a problem before trying to solve it. You can do this by verbalizing or drawing the steps, or by using real objects. This is the easiest, yet least fun, part of problem-solving!

ASK "HOW DID YOU DO IT?"

Gradually help them get accustomed to verbalizing and explaining their thinking processes; it is far more important for them to know how they thought it through and why, rather than knowing the name of the rule they used.

The situations proposed in this book are of course imaginary.
Help your child track down numbers, measurements,
and math in general in their everyday life.
Get your nose out of the book, and go and meet mathematics!

THE BIGGEST ANIMALS THAT EVER EXISTED!

THAT IS WHAT'S KNOWN ABOUT US DINOSAURS, BUT WHAT EXACTLY DOES "BIG" MEAN? IT'S A BIT GENERIC! TAKE A LOOK AT ME AND MY FRIENDS— WE ARE DINO PUPS, BUT SOME OF US ARE ALREADY CONSIDERED BIG BECAUSE WE ARE REALLY HEAVY, WHILE OTHERS ARE REALLY TALL.

DINO

WE NEED YOUR HELP TO FIND OUT MORE. THAT'S WHY WE HAVE DECIDED TO INVADE YOU! NOTHING TO WORRY ABOUT, REALLY! WE JUST TRAVELED IN TIME TO UNDERSTAND HOW YOU, AN EVOLVED RACE, MEASURE YOUR WORLD! THERE ARE FIVE OF US; HERE ARE MY FRIENDS:

TRIXIE

STEGGIE

BRONTO

TERRI

IN A FEW YEARS, WE WILL GROW AND BECOME "BIG." A T-REX LIKE ME, BUT ADULT SIZED, IS ABOUT 16'5" **TALL**, FOR EXAMPLE. SO, IF YOU WERE ON THE THIRD FLOOR OF A BUILDING, I COULD LOOK STRAIGHT AT YOU THROUGH THE WINDOW.

16'5 FT

THE STEGOSAURUS IS ABOUT 30 FEET **LONG**. THAT MEANS IT'S EASILY THE SIZE OF A SCHOOL BUS OR A VOLLEYBALL COURT.

30 FT

OVER TIME, YOU HUMANS HAVE DISCOVERED RULES FOR MEASURING NOT ONLY **LENGTH**, BUT ALSO **TIME**, **TEMPERATURE**, AND THE **WEIGHT**, **SIZE**, AND **CAPACITY** OF EVERYTHING THAT SURROUNDS YOU. AND WE ARE HERE TO LEARN HOW YOU DO IT! THIS IS HOW WE ARE GOING TO SPLIT UP...

TERRI WILL TAKE CARE OF **LENGTHS** AND **SURFACES**

STEGGIE WILL TAKE CARE OF **CAPACITY**

BRONTO WILL TAKE CARE OF **MASS**

LET'S START!

DINO WILL TAKE CARE OF **TEMPERATURE**

TRIXIE WILL TAKE CARE OF **TIME**

5

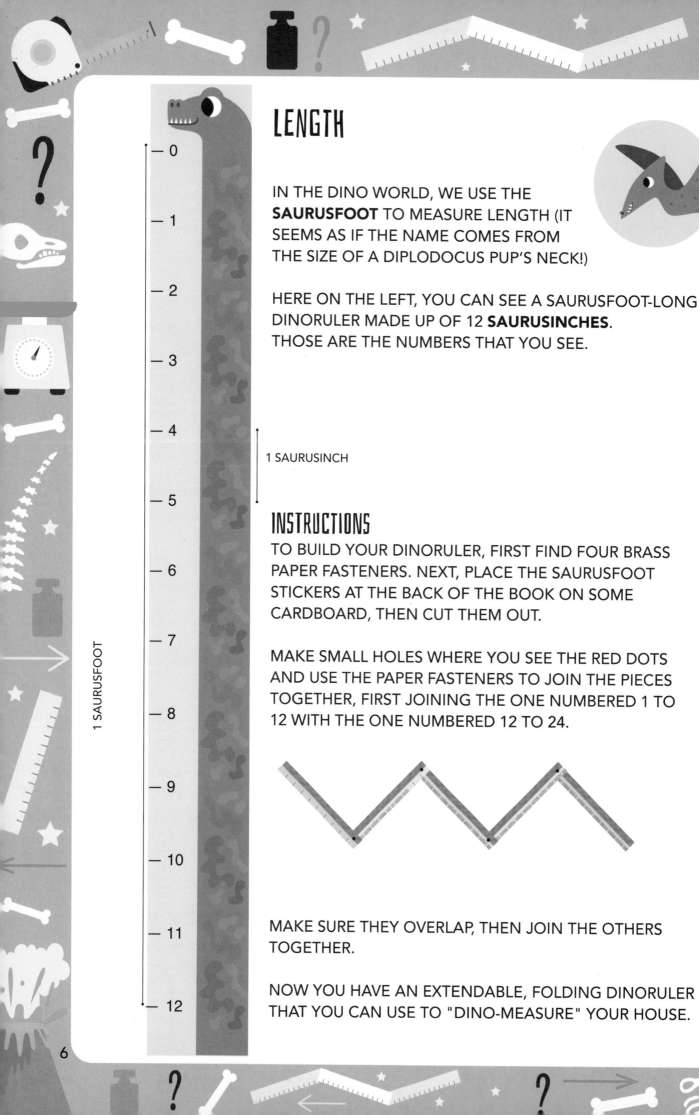

LENGTH

IN THE DINO WORLD, WE USE THE **SAURUSFOOT** TO MEASURE LENGTH (IT SEEMS AS IF THE NAME COMES FROM THE SIZE OF A DIPLODOCUS PUP'S NECK!)

HERE ON THE LEFT, YOU CAN SEE A SAURUSFOOT-LONG DINORULER MADE UP OF 12 **SAURUSINCHES**. THOSE ARE THE NUMBERS THAT YOU SEE.

1 SAURUSINCH

INSTRUCTIONS

TO BUILD YOUR DINORULER, FIRST FIND FOUR BRASS PAPER FASTENERS. NEXT, PLACE THE SAURUSFOOT STICKERS AT THE BACK OF THE BOOK ON SOME CARDBOARD, THEN CUT THEM OUT.

MAKE SMALL HOLES WHERE YOU SEE THE RED DOTS AND USE THE PAPER FASTENERS TO JOIN THE PIECES TOGETHER, FIRST JOINING THE ONE NUMBERED 1 TO 12 WITH THE ONE NUMBERED 12 TO 24.

MAKE SURE THEY OVERLAP, THEN JOIN THE OTHERS TOGETHER.

NOW YOU HAVE AN EXTENDABLE, FOLDING DINORULER THAT YOU CAN USE TO "DINO-MEASURE" YOUR HOUSE.

1 SAURUSFOOT

0
1
2
3
4
5
6
7
8
9
10
11
12

MEASURE YOUR WORLD IN SAURUSFEET!

START TAKING YOUR MEASUREMENTS:

HOW WIDE IS THE DOOR TO YOUR BEDROOM?

_____

HOW LONG IS YOUR TABLE?

_____

HOW HIGH IS YOUR WINDOW?

_____

HOW MANY SAURUSFEET IS YOUR
BED FROM THE FLOOR?

_____

NOW THAT YOU HAVE USED YOUR DINORULER TO MEASURE THINGS AROUND YOUR HOME, USE IT TO FIND THE OBJECTS THAT ARE EQUAL TO **4 SAURUSINCHES** IN THIS GARDEN.

OUR ANCESTORS INVENTED LOTS OF DIFFERENT AND INGENIOUS METHODS TO MEASURE LENGTHS.
ONCE UPON A TIME, FOR EXAMPLE, WE USED PALMS, INCHES, CUBITS (FOREARMS), AND FEET.

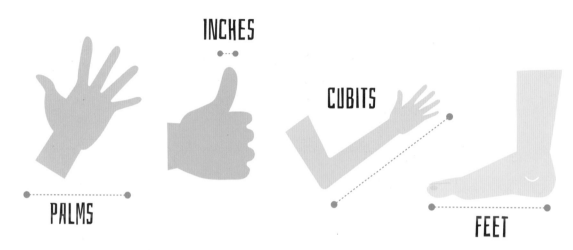

INCHES

CUBITS

PALMS

FEET

THEN, OVER TIME, WE CAME TO ADOPT WHAT IS CALLED THE UNITED STATES CUSTOMARY SYSTEM, WHICH KEPT SOME OF THESE MEASUREMENTS—LIKE **FEET** AND **INCHES**—TO MEASURE LENGTH.

IN ORDER TO MEASURE SMALLER AND BIGGER THINGS, WE NEED TO USE SOME MULTIPLES AND SUBDIVISIONS OF A FOOT...

LOOK AT THE KEY BELOW AND USE THE CODE TO FIGURE OUT THE NAMES OF MULTIPLES AND SUBDIVISIONS OF A FOOT.

KEY

D	M	I	Y	C	E	R	S	L	H	N	A
1	2	3	4	5	6	7	8	9	10	11	12

WHAT IS THE MEASUREMENT EQUAL TO 3 FEET CALLED?

$$\overline{}_4 \quad \overline{}_{12} \quad \overline{}_7 \quad \overline{}_1$$

1 FOOT IS MADE UP OF 12 WHAT?

$$\overline{}_3 \quad \overline{}_{11} \quad \overline{}_5 \quad \overline{}_{10} \quad \overline{}_6 \quad \overline{}_8$$

WHAT ARE 1,760 YARDS CALLED?

$$\overline{}_2 \quad \overline{}_3 \quad \overline{}_9 \quad \overline{}_6$$

THERE ARE LOTS OF THINGS TO MEASURE IN YOUR TOWN.
USE THE KEY TO ADD TOGETHER THE DIFFERENT MEASUREMENTS THAT TERRI TOOK.

◆ = 1 INCH
◎ = 1 FOOT
★ = 1 YARD
🦴 = 1 MILE

◎◎◎◎◎◆◆◆
CAR

🦴★★★★◎◎◎◎◎◎◎◆◆◆◆◆◆
BRIDGE

◆◆◆◆◆◆◆◆◆◆◆◆◆◆◆◆◆◆◎◎
BENCH

🦴🦴★★★★★◆◆◆◆◆◆◆◆◆◆◆◆◆◆◆◆◆
RIVER

Symbol	Value
🌙	= 1/4 INCH
⬡	= 1/2 INCH
⬤	= 3/4 INCH
♥	= 1 INCH

A 7.5 SIZE SHOE

A US DOLLAR BILL

A MAPLE LEAF

A PLASTIC SPOON

DIAMETER OF A BASEBALL

TOY TRAIN

STEGGIE AND **TRIXIE** ARE EXPLORING THE CITY.

HELP TERRI WORK OUT HOW FAR THEY HAVE WALKED.

BAKERY

STEGGIE IS ONE FOOT FROM THE BAKERY, WHICH IS 10 YARDS FROM THE FRUIT AND VEGETABLE STORE. HOW MANY FEET WILL HE HAVE WALKED WHEN HE HAS PASSED THEM BOTH?

ICE CREAM PARLOR

TRIXIE IS 10 YARDS FROM THE FLORIST, 5 YARDS FROM THE PASTRY SHOP, AND 3 FEET FROM THE ICE CREAM PARLOR.

SHE WOULD LIKE TO TASTE SOME CAKES, BUT ALSO EAT SOME ICE CREAM.
HOW FAR WILL SHE HAVE TO WALK IN INCHES?

TERRI IS FLYING OVER THE TOWN TO GIVE **DINO** DIRECTIONS. TO UNDERSTAND EACH OTHER, THEY HAVE DIVIDED THE TOWN INTO SQUARES OF 1 FOOT.

FOLLOWING TERRI'S DIRECTIONS, WHERE WILL DINO END UP?

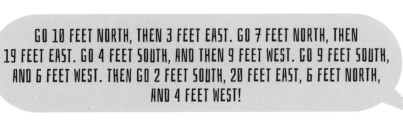

GO 10 FEET NORTH, THEN 3 FEET EAST. GO 7 FEET NORTH, THEN 19 FEET EAST. GO 4 FEET SOUTH, AND THEN 9 FEET WEST. GO 9 FEET SOUTH, AND 6 FEET WEST. THEN GO 2 FEET SOUTH, 20 FEET EAST, 6 FEET NORTH, AND 4 FEET WEST!

FLYING OVER THE CITY, **TERRI** DRAWS EVERY BUILDING SO THAT
MEASURING THE AREAS OF ALL THE BUILDINGS IS SIMPLE.

HOW MANY HOUSES OCCUPY AN AREA OF 4 SQUARES?
HOW MANY BUILDINGS OCCUPY AN AREA OF 16 SQUARES?

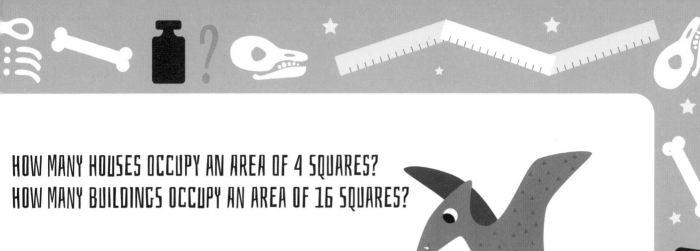

THE DINO PUPS LOVE PLAYING A GAME THAT RESEMBLES BATTLESHIP.

TERRI IS A REAL CHAMPION, AND HE HAS DISCOVERED, THANKS TO THE AREA, HOW MANY TIMES HE HAS TO HIT HIS ENEMY IN ORDER TO SINK THE SHIPS! WHAT'S HIS SECRET? JUST CALCULATE THE AREA OF THE FLEET. WHY DON'T YOU TRY: HOW MANY SQUARES CORRESPOND TO THE AREA OF ALL THE SHIPS?

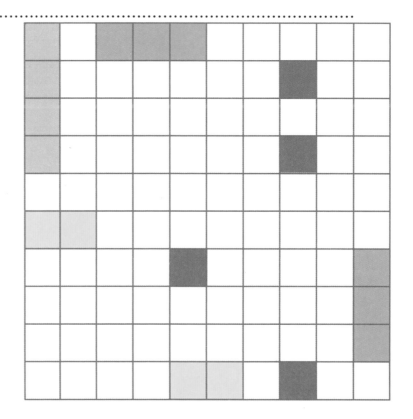

AIRCRAFT CARRIER

BATTLE CRUISER

TORPEDO BOAT

SUBMARINE

PLAY BATTLESHIP WITH A FRIEND.

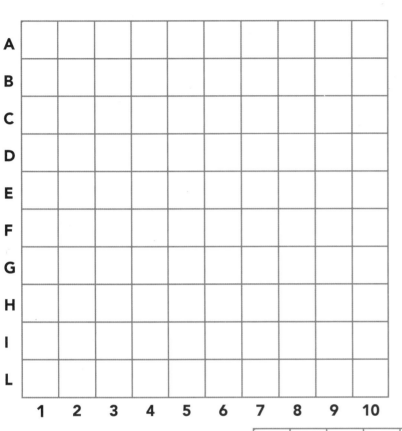

BUT MAKE SURE
YOU KEEP YOUR BATTLE
GRID SECRET!

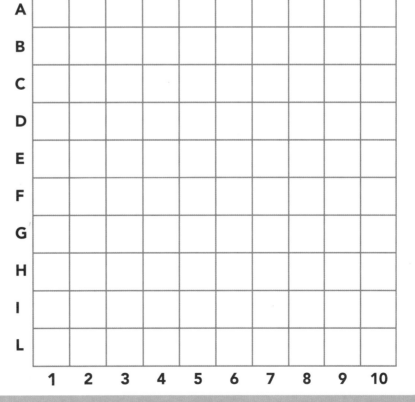

ANOTHER GAME THAT TERRI LOVES IS **PENTOMINO PUZZLES**. A PENTOMIN
IS A SHAPE MADE UP OF 5 SQUARES, WHICH ARE ALL THE SAME SIZE AND
ARE JOINED ON AT LEAST ONE SIDE. THERE ARE 12 PENTOMINOES IN TOTA

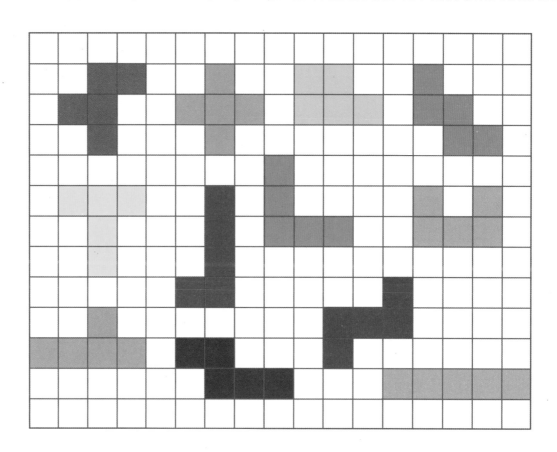

CAN YOU FIT THEM ALL IN A RECTANGLE WITH AN AREA OF 6X10 SQUARES?

THERE ARE A TOTAL OF 2,339 ANSWERS! TERRI FOUND ONE, WHICH
YOU CAN FIND AT THE END OF THE BOOK. COMPARE IT WITH YOURS.
USE A PENCIL, BUT DRAW LIGHTLY SO THAT YOU CAN EASILY ERASE IT
AND TRY AGAIN.

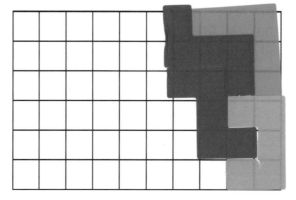

USING PENTOMINOES, YOU CAN DISCOVER LOTS OF STRANGE SHAPES. CAN YOU USE THEM ALL TO COMPLETE THESE IMAGES?

USE THE STICKERS AT THE BACK OF THE BOOK AND FIND OUT WHAT ANIMALS THEY PORTRAY.

THE ANIMALS MADE UP OF PENTOMINOES HAVE THE SAME AREA.

CAN YOU WORK IT OUT?

....

MASS

THE **SAURUSPOUND** IS THE MEASUREMENT DINOSAURS USE TO MEASURE MASS. THERE IS A GREAT DEBATE AMONG THEM ABOUT WHO WEIGHS THE MOST SAURUSPOUNDS! USING THE THREE STATEMENTS BELOW, CAN YOU PUT THE DINOSAURS IN ORDER OF **WEIGHT**, FROM THE HEAVIEST TO THE LIGHTEST?

USE THE STICKERS WITH THE PICTURES OF THE DINOSAURS AT THE BACK OF THE BOOK TO GIVE THE RIGHT ANSWER.

1. TERRI WEIGHS A LOT LESS SAURUSPOUNDS THAN STEGGIE.
2. DINO WEIGHS LESS THAN BRONTO, BUT MORE THAN STEGGIE.
3. TRIXIE WEIGHS MORE SAURUSPOUNDS THAN STEGGIE AND LESS THAN DINO.

MASS IS THE QUANTITY OF MATTER THAT BODIES AND OBJECTS ARE MADE UP OF; IT IS A PROPERTY OF OBJECTS AND LIVING THINGS.
WEIGHT IS THE FORCE WITH WHICH A BODY IS ATTRACTED TO THE EARTH; WEIGHT IS THE VALUE OF THE **FORCE OF GRAVITY** THAT IS EXERCISED ON THE MASS.

IN EVERYDAY LANGUAGE, WE TEND TO CONFUSE THE TWO THINGS. FOR EXAMPLE, WE HAVE THE SAME MASS ON THE EARTH AS ON THE MOON, BUT WE HAVE A DIFFERENT WEIGHT BECAUSE THIS IS SUBJECT TO TWO DIFFERENT FORCES OF GRAVITY: EARTH'S AND THE MOON'S. ON THE MOON, FOR EXAMPLE, WE WOULD WEIGH ABOUT ONE-SIXTH LESS!

IF BRONTO WEIGHED 600 LBS ON EARTH...

...ON THE MOON HE WOULD HAVE THE SAME MASS, BUT HE WOULD ONLY WEIGH ABOUT 100 LBS.

WE EXPRESS **MASS** IN THE US CUSTOMARY SYSTEM IN **POUNDS**, WHEREAS IN MANY PARTS OF THE WORLD THEY USE **GRAMS**. THIS TYPE OF MEASUREMENT IS VERY USEFUL, BUT OUR SYSTEM HAS ONLY A FEW SUBDIVISIONS COMPARED TO THE METRIC SYSTEM. THAT IS WHY, UNTIL A FEW YEARS AGO, WE USED THE **APOTHECARIES' SYSTEM** TO MEASURE VERY SMALL WEIGHTS.

SUBDIVISIONS

16 DRAMS = 1 OUNCE
16 OUNCES = 1 LB

MULTIPLES

A HUNDREDWEIGHT = 100 LBS
A TON = 2,000 LBS

WE NEED THE APOTHECARIES' SYSTEM TO MEASURE **LIGHTER** OBJECTS. TRY AND GUESS WHICH OBJECTS WEIGH LESS THAN AN OUNCE.

FIND THE CORRESPONDING STICKERS AT THE BACK OF THE BOOK TO REVEAL THE MYSTERIOUS OBJECTS!

DRAM

→

SCRUPLES

→

GRAINS

→

0.1 GRAIN

→

MULTIPLES OF POUNDS ARE USED TO MEASURE HEAVIER OBJECTS. FLYING OVER THE CITY, **STEGGIE** SAW SOME OBJECTS WITH VERY DIFFERENT MASSES.

STARTING AT THE LEAST HEAVIEST OBJECT, DRAW A LINE TO THE NEXT HEAVIEST OBJECT, AND CONTINUE DRAWING LINES THIS WAY UNTIL YOU REACH THE HEAVIEST OBJECT—WITHOUT EVER CROSSING OVER YOUR LINE.

1 TON

2.5 POUNDS

3 OUNCES

DRAM

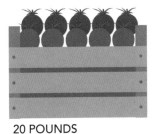

20 POUNDS

200 POUNDS

BRONTO CAN EAT A LOT OF FRUIT! EXPLORING THE CITY, HE FOUND A REALLY GOOD FRUIT AND VEGETABLE STORE. THE OWNER PUT HIS ENORMOUS BASKETS OF FRUIT ON 3 SCALES, BUT NOW HE CAN'T SEEM TO MAKE THEM BALANCE. THE WEIGHTS THAT YOU CAN USE ARE:

9 X 1 OUNCE (OZ) WEIGHTS   13 X 1 POUND (LB) WEIGHTS

IF YOU KNOW THE WEIGHT OF TWO BASKETS, CAN YOU CALCULATE HOW MUCH THE THIRD ONE WEIGHS?

....

DISTRIBUTE THE STICKERS ON THE THREE SCALES, SO AS TO MAKE THEM BALANCE.

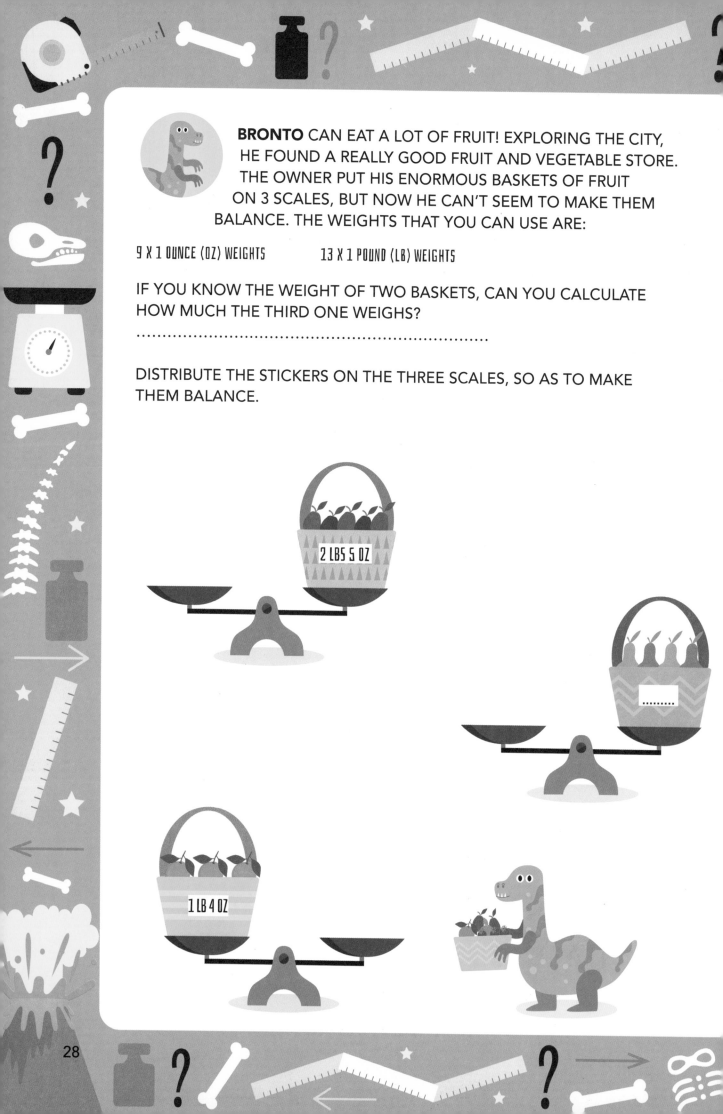

2 LBS 5 OZ

1 LB 4 OZ

HERE IN THE US, WE USE **TEASPOONS**, **TABLESPOONS**, AND **CUPS** TO WEIGH INGREDIENTS, WHEREAS IN EUROPE THEY HAVE A DIFFERENT SYSTEM. CAN YOU HELP THAT HUNGRY BRONTO MAKE THIS CAKE RECIPE? YOU CAN HELP HIM BY CONVERTING THE MEASUREMENTS, KNOWING THAT:

1 TEASPOON IS EQUAL TO 4 GRAMS
1 TABLESPOON IS EQUAL TO 12 GRAMS
1 CUP IS EQUAL TO 16 TEASPOONS

CAN YOU CONVERT THE RECIPE INTO GRAMS?

SIMPLE CAKE

INGREDIENTS:

---------------------- 1 CUP SUGAR

---------------------- 8 TEASPOONS BUTTER

2 EGGS

---------------------- 2 TEASPOONS VANILLA EXTRACT

---------------------- 1 AND A HALF CUPS FLOUR

---------------------- 1 AND A HALF TEASPOONS BAKING POWDER

---------------------- 8 TEASPOONS OF MILK

PREHEAT THE OVEN TO 350°F. • BUTTER AN 8-INCH CAKEPAN. • IN A BOWL, MIX SUGAR AND BUTTER TOGETHER. • WHISK IN THE EGGS ONE AT A TIME, AND ADD THE VANILLA EXTRACT. • ADD THE FLOUR AND THE BAKING POWDER AND MIX WELL. • ADD THE MILK UNTIL YOU GET A SMOOTH, CREAMY MIXTURE, THEN POUR IT INTO THE CAKEPAN AND COOK IN THE OVEN FOR 30 MINUTES AT 350°F.

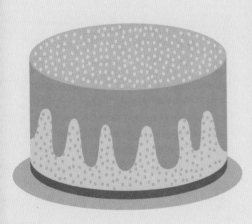

CAPACITY

STEGGIE IS VERY THIRSTY; SHE COULD REALLY USE **FIVE SAURUSPINTS** OF WATER! THE **SAURUSPINT** (WHICH WAS INVENTED BY THE DINO PUPS) MEASURES CAPACITY, WHICH IS THE QUANTITY OF LIQUID THAT A CONTAINER CAN HOLD.

IF A SAURUSPINT IS MADE UP OF 2 CUPS, FIGURE OUT HOW MANY CUPS STEGGIE NEEDS TO QUENCH HER THIRST.

HUMANS DON'T USE SAURUSPINTS; INSTEAD THEY USE A
UNIT OF MEASUREMENT CALLED **LITERS**. THE LITER HAS...

SUBDIVISIONS

DECILITER = 0.1 LITERS
CENTILITER = 0.01 LITERS
MILLILITER = 0.001 LITERS

MULTIPLES

DECALITER = 10 LITERS
HECTOLITER = 100 LITERS
KILOLITER = 1,000 LITERS

USE THE STICKERS AT THE BACK OF THE BOOK TO MATCH THE CAPACITY WITH THE RIGHT CONTAINER.

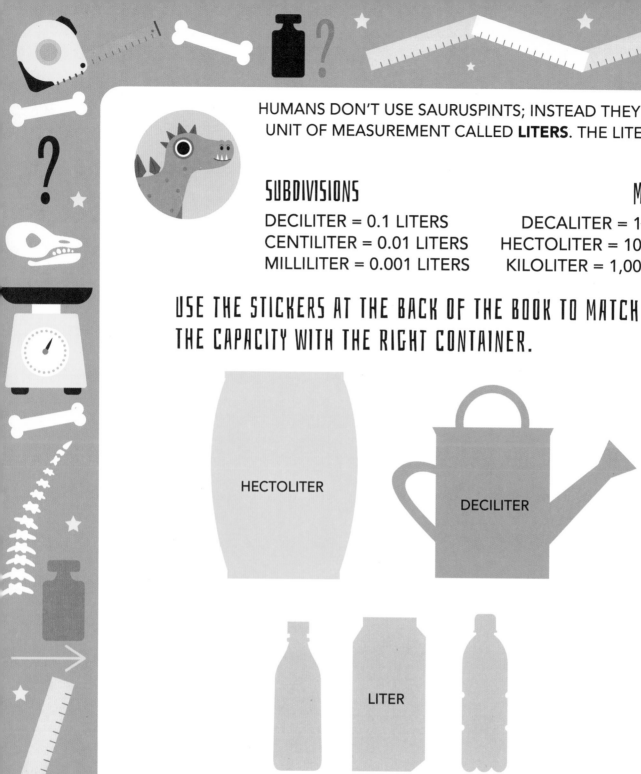

HECTOLITER

DECILITER

LITER

CENTILITER

MILLILITER

STEGGIE HAS DISCOVERED THAT NOT EVERYONE USES THE SAME SYSTEM TO MEASURE LIQUIDS. IN THE UNITED STATES, THERE IS A DIFFERENT WAY TO MEASURE THE VOLUME AND CAPACITY OF LIQUIDS. THESE MEASUREMENTS ARE CALLED CUPS, PINTS, QUARTS, AND GALLONS.

HELP STEGGIE UNDERSTAND HOW TO CONVERT THE MEASUREMENTS.

CUP + CUP = PINT

PINT + PINT = QUART

QUART + QUART + QUART + QUART = GALLON

HOW MANY PINTS ARE 13 CUPS? ....

HOW MANY QUARTS ARE 9 PINTS? ....

HOW MANY GALLONS ARE 7 QUARTS? ....

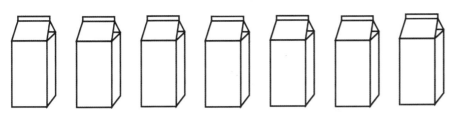

TIME

TRIXIE HAS DISCOVERED THAT TO MEASURE **TIME**, WE CALCULATE THE INTERVAL BETWEEN PRECISE MOMENTS. TRIXIE IS A BIT CONFUSED (DINOSAURS ARE USED TO COUNTING MILLIONS OF YEARS AT A TIME), SO LET'S TRY AND HELP HER!

WHAT INTERVAL OF TIME CAN BEST BE MEASURED WITH EACH OF THESE OBJECTS?
DRAW A LINE BETWEEN THE OBJECT AND THE TIME INTERVAL.

HOURGLASS

PENDULUM

STOPWATCH

SECONDS

MINUTES

HOURS

LOOK AT THE TABLES CAREFULLY!
60 SECONDS = **1 MINUTE**
60 MINUTES = **1 HOUR**
24 HOURS = **1 DAY!**

SECONDS

1	2	3	4	5	6	7	8	9	10
11	12	13	14	15	16	17	18	19	20
21	22	23	24	25	26	27	28	29	30
31	32	33	34	35	36	37	38	39	40
41	42	43	44	45	46	47	48	49	50
51	52	53	54	55	56	57	58	59	60

IN ADDITION:
7 DAYS = **1 WEEK**
FROM 28 TO 31 DAYS =
1 MONTH
365 DAYS = **1 YEAR**

(EXCEPT FOR ONE IN EVERY
FOUR YEARS, WHICH IS CALLED
A LEAP YEAR AND CONSISTS
OF 366 DAYS)

MINUTES

1	2	3	4	5	6	7	8	9	10
11	12	13	14	15	16	17	18	19	20
21	22	23	24	25	26	27	28	29	30
31	32	33	34	35	36	37	38	39	40
41	42	43	44	45	46	47	48	49	50
51	52	53	54	55	56	57	58	59	60

HOURS

1	2	3	4	5	6
7	8	9	10	11	12
13	14	15	16	17	18
19	20	21	22	23	24

WHAT COMES AFTER A YEAR?
5 YEARS = **1 LUSTRUM (HALF A DECADE)**
10 YEARS = **1 DECADE**
100 YEARS = **1 CENTURY**
1,000 YEARS = **1 MILLENNIUM**

A TRULY SPECIAL PLACE THAT COULD HELP TRIXIE SORT OUT HER CONFUSION IS THE CLOCK MUSEUM. CLOCKS ARE THE TOOLS THAT WE USE TO MEASURE **TIME**.

HELP TRIXIE READ THE TIME ON EACH CLOCK. REMEMBER THAT THE SHORT HAND IS FOR HOURS AND THE LONG HAND IS FOR MINUTES.

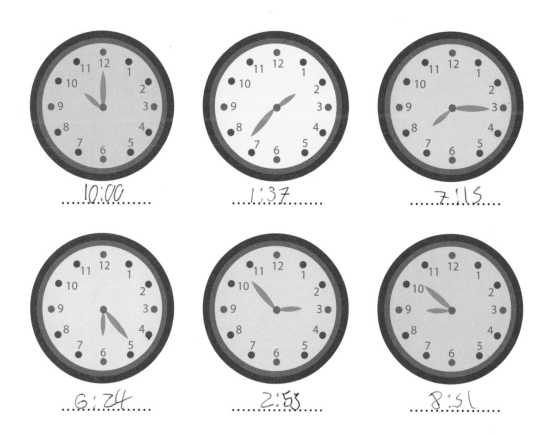

10:00

1:37

7:15

6:24

2:53

8:51

DRAW THE HANDS IN THE RIGHT PLACES.

4:23

12:47

10:02

MATCH THE WATCHES AND CLOCKS BELOW TO THE DIGITAL CLOCKS IN THE STICKER SECTION OF THE BOOK. BE CAREFUL: CHOOSE THE ONES THAT SHOW THE SAME TIME!

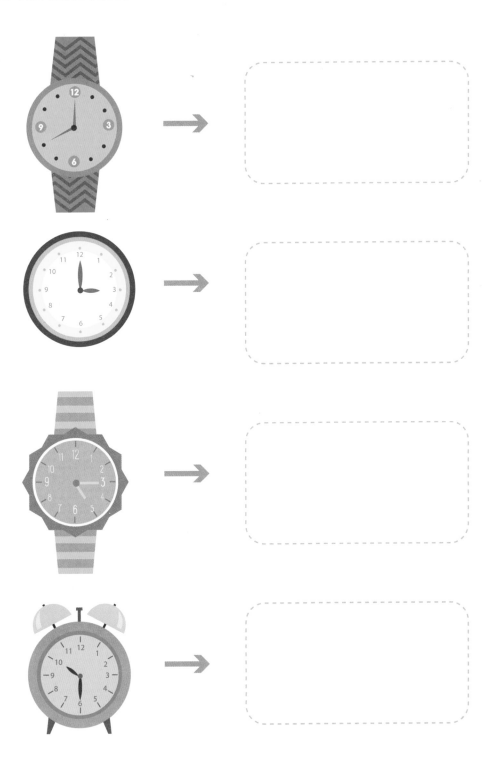

LET'S SEE IF, THANKS TO YOUR HELP, TRIXIE NOW
UNDERSTANDS HOW A CLOCK WORKS.

HELP TRIXIE ANSWER THE QUESTION NEXT TO EACH CLOCK.

TIME:

HOW MANY MINUTES
HAVE PASSED SINCE 8:45?

....
....

TIME:

HOW MANY MINUTES
HAVE PASSED SINCE 3:30?

....
....

TIME:

HOW MANY MINUTES
HAVE PASSED SINCE 5:15?

....
....

ANSWER THESE QUESIONS WITH THE STICKERS FROM THE BACK OF THE BOOK.

WHAT TIME IS IT NOW?

....

WHAT TIME
WILL IT BE
IN 15 MINUTES?

→

WHAT TIME IS IT NOW?

....

WHAT TIME
WILL IT BE
IN 9 HOURS?

→

WHAT TIME IS IT NOW?

....

WHAT TIME
WILL IT BE
IN 45 MINUTES?

→

TEMPERATURE

IT'S REALLY HOT TODAY! HOW CAN WE MEASURE HOW HOT IT IS, IN AN EXACT WAY? TEMPERATURE IS MEASURED IN DEGREES, WITH TWO SCALES: ONE TAKES ITS NAME FROM THE SWEDISH SCIENTIST **ANDERS CELSIUS**, AND THE SECOND IS CALLED **THE FAHRENHEIT SCALE**, IN HONOR OF THE GERMAN PHYSICIST DANIEL GABRIEL FAHRENHEIT.

> ## TO CONVERT TEMPERATURE FROM FAHRENHEIT TO CELSIUS, YOU HAVE TO SUBTRACT 32 AND DIVIDE BY 1.8:
> $$(°F - 32) \div 1.8 = °C$$

IT LOOKS DIFFICULT, UNTIL YOU TRY.
HERE IS A STEP-BY-STEP EXAMPLE:

86°F - 32 = 54   54 ÷ 1.8 = 30°C

ATTACH THE STICKER SHOWING THE CORRECT TEMPERATURE IN FAHRENHEIT UNDER THE THERMOMETER SHOWING THE CORRESPONDING TEMPERATURE IN DEGREES CELSIUS.

25°C

80°C

5°C

WATCH OUT, DINO! IN A HUMAN KITCHEN YOU CAN FIND VERY
LOW TEMPERATURES, BUT ALSO VERY HIGH ONES!

FIGURE OUT AT WHAT TEMPERATURE WATER BOILS OR FREEZES BY CONVERTING THE MEASUREMENTS FROM FAHRENHEIT TO DEGREES CELSIUS.

WELCOME TO THE DINOLYMPICS!

THE DINO PUPS HAVE BEEN STUDYING THE UNITS OF MEASUREMENT CAREFULLY, AND NOW EACH ONE THINKS THEY KNOW MORE THAN THE OTHERS. HOW DO WE FIND OUT? WITH THE **DINOLYMPICS** OF COURSE! THROUGH A VARIETY OF COMPETITIONS, THEY WILL PUT THEMSELVES TO THE TEST AND REVISIT EVERYTHING THEY HAVE LEARNED SO FAR. LET'S BEGIN!

HOW MANY INCHES WILL TERRI TRAVEL IF WE ADD TOGETHER ALL THE MEASUREMENTS IN THE 5 BOXES BELOW?

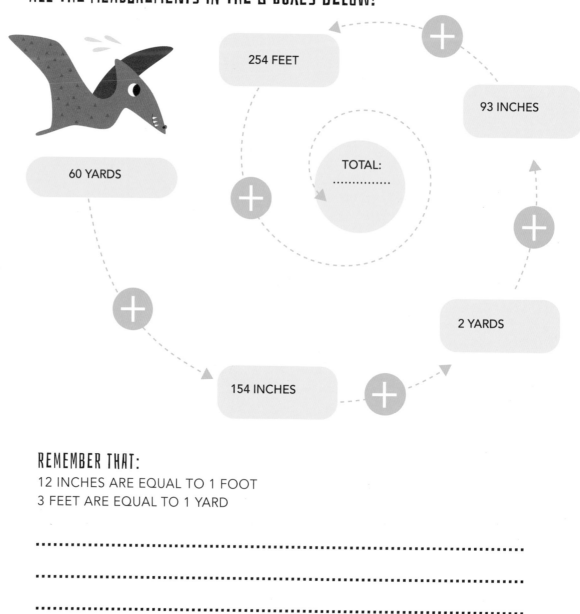

254 FEET

93 INCHES

60 YARDS

TOTAL:
....

2 YARDS

154 INCHES

REMEMBER THAT:
12 INCHES ARE EQUAL TO 1 FOOT
3 FEET ARE EQUAL TO 1 YARD

....

....

....

NOW THEY ARE ALL INVOLVED. THE REAL RACE HAS BEGUN!

IF YOU KNOW HOW LONG EACH DINOSAUR TOOK TO COMPLETE THE RACE, CAN YOU WORK OUT HOW MANY SECONDS IN TOTAL IT TOOK THEM TO FINISH?

REMEMBER THAT:
60 SECONDS ARE EQUAL TO 1 MINUTE
1,000 MILLISECONDS ARE EQUAL TO 1 SECOND

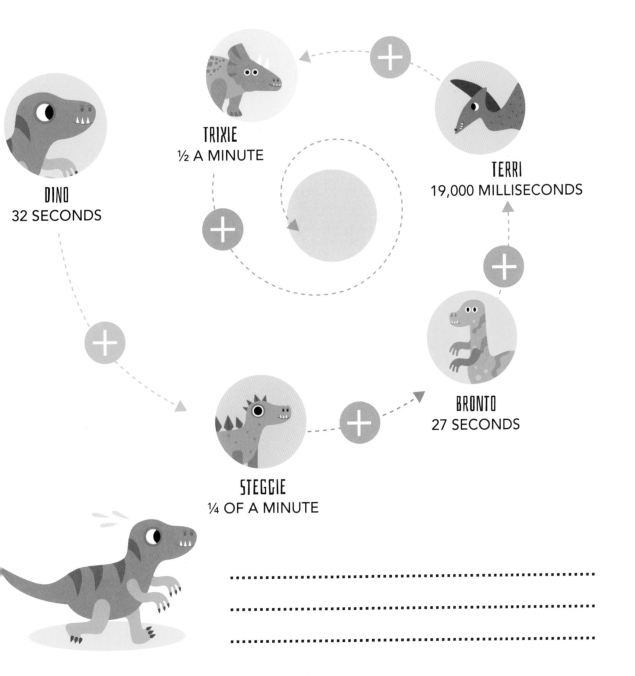

DINO
32 SECONDS

TRIXIE
½ A MINUTE

TERRI
19,000 MILLISECONDS

BRONTO
27 SECONDS

STEGGIE
¼ OF A MINUTE

....

....

....

NOW IS THE TIME FOR THE DINOSAURS TO PROVE THEIR STRENGTH. THE DINOLYMPICS WEIGHTLIFTING COMPETITION IS ABOUT TO BEGIN!

HOW MANY POUNDS IS EACH DINOSAUR LIFTING?

31 LBS + 4,352 OZ
+ 203 DRAMS =

....

....

55 LBS + 864 OZ =

....

....

77 LBS + 700 DRAMS =

....

....

BRONTO

STEGGIE

DINO

ATTACH THE DINOSAUR STICKERS IN THE RIGHT PLACE ON THE PODIUM.

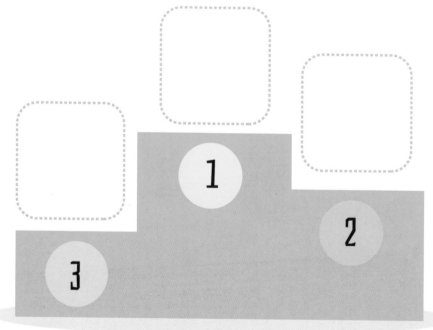

ATTACH THE STICKER WITH THE CORRECT ANSWER TO EACH QUESTION.

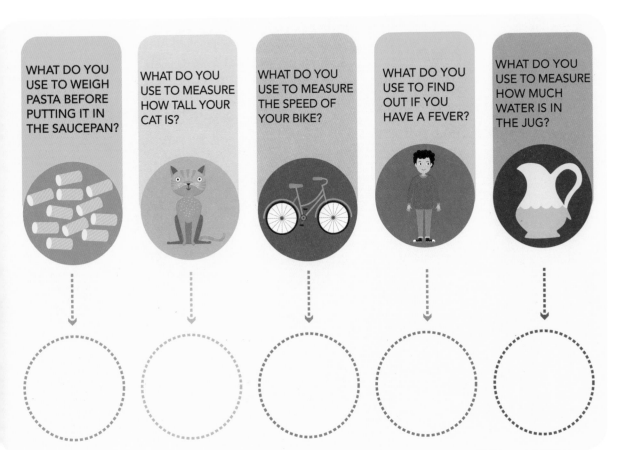

WHAT DO YOU USE TO WEIGH PASTA BEFORE PUTTING IT IN THE SAUCEPAN?

WHAT DO YOU USE TO MEASURE HOW TALL YOUR CAT IS?

WHAT DO YOU USE TO MEASURE THE SPEED OF YOUR BIKE?

WHAT DO YOU USE TO FIND OUT IF YOU HAVE A FEVER?

WHAT DO YOU USE TO MEASURE HOW MUCH WATER IS IN THE JUG?

MATCH THE OBJECTS TO WHAT THEY MEASURE.

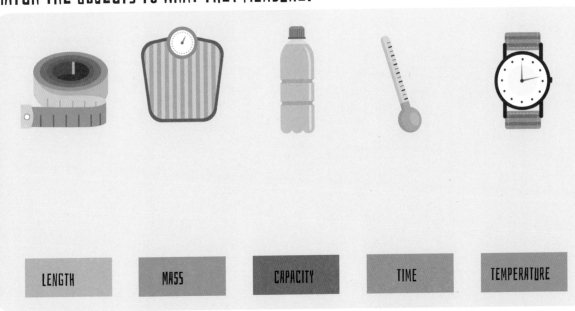

 LENGTH

MASS

CAPACITY

 TIME

 TEMPERATURE

THE DINOLYMPICS END IN SOME CONFUSION...

WHICH IS THE ODD MEASUREMENT OUT IN EACH DINOSAUR'S BALLOON?

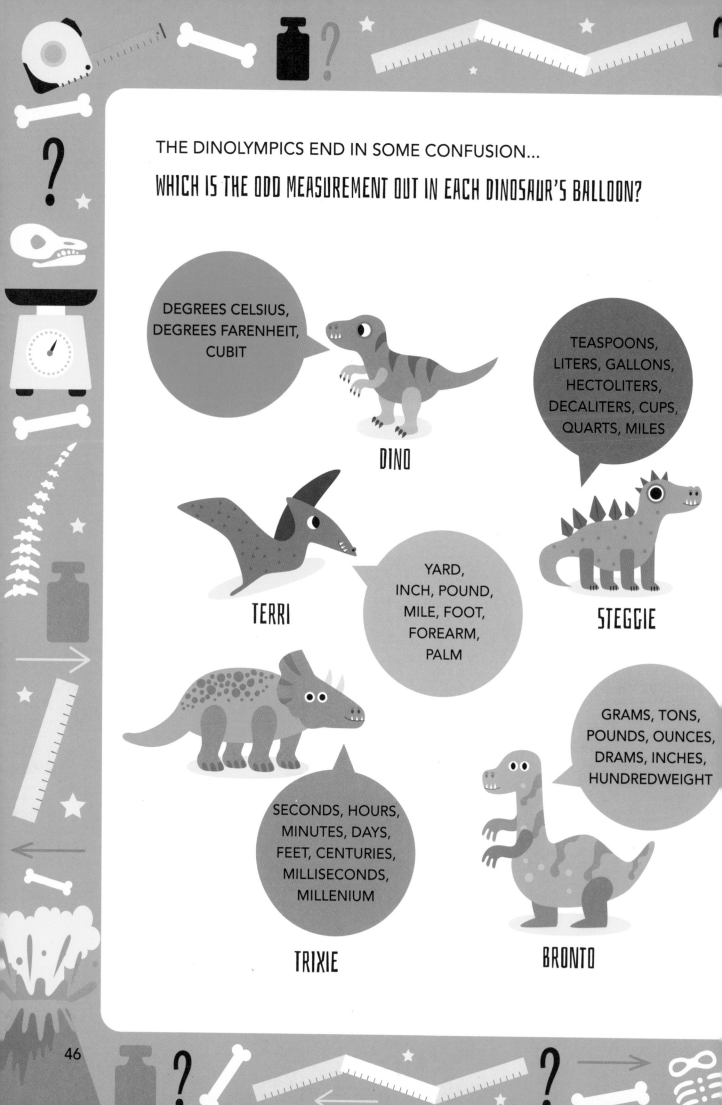

DEGREES CELSIUS, DEGREES FARENHEIT, CUBIT

DINO

TEASPOONS, LITERS, GALLONS, HECTOLITERS, DECALITERS, CUPS, QUARTS, MILES

STEGGIE

TERRI

YARD, INCH, POUND, MILE, FOOT, FOREARM, PALM

GRAMS, TONS, POUNDS, OUNCES, DRAMS, INCHES, HUNDREDWEIGHT

SECONDS, HOURS, MINUTES, DAYS, FEET, CENTURIES, MILLISECONDS, MILLENIUM

TRIXIE

BRONTO

DINO-DOMINOES

HERE IS THE KEY TO THE SYMBOLS ON
EACH OF THE DOMINO TILES BELOW:

 TIME
 MASS
 LENGTH
 CAPACITY
 TEMPERATURE

ATTACH THE THREE MISSING DOMINOES IN THE CORRECT PLACES USING THE STICKERS.

MAKE SURE YOU MATCH
THE SYMBOLS ON THE STICKERS TO
THE DOMINOES CORRECLY!

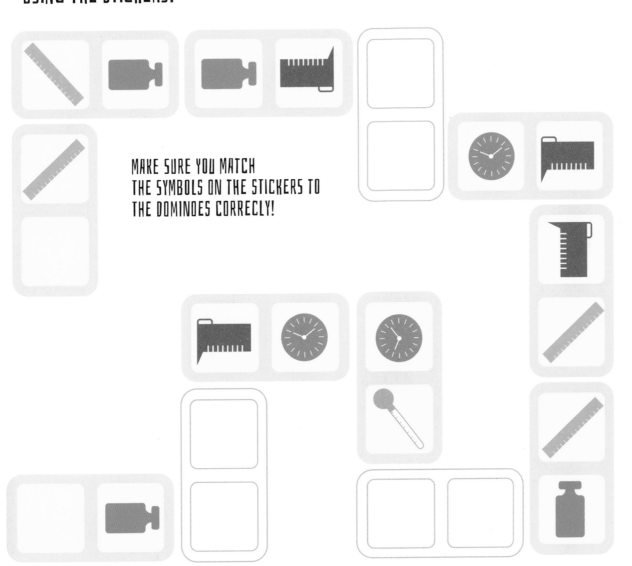

THAT'S NOT ALL!

IN ADDITION TO THE MEASUREMENTS THAT YOU HAVE EXPLORED, THERE ARE OTHER THINGS TO MEASURE. EACH HAS ITS OWN PIECE OF EQUIPMENT. HERE ARE SOME EXAMPLES.

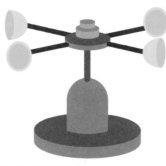

THE INSTRUMENT FOR MEASURING **WIND** SPEED IS CALLED AN **ANEMOMETER**.

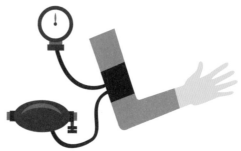

THE INSTRUMENT USED FOR MEASURING **BLOOD PRESSURE** IS CALLED A **SPHYGMOMANOMETER**.

THE INSTRUMENT USED FOR MEASURING **ANGLES** IS CALLED A **PROTRACTOR**.

THE TIRE PRESSURE GAUGE, OR **MANOMETER**, IS USED TO MEASURE THE **PRESSURE** IN YOUR BICYCLE OR CAR TIRES.

THE INSTRUMENT THAT IS USED TO MEASURE **SPEED** IS CALLED A **SPEEDOMETER**.

SCIENTISTS USE A **SEISMOGRAPH** TO MEASURE THE FORCE OF **EARTHQUAKES**.

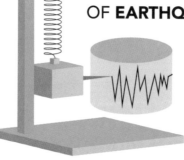

LET'S "MEASURE" SOME WORDS!

HELP TRIXIE SOLVE THE CROSSWORD.

DOWN
1. DEVICE THAT MEASURES BLOOD PRESSURE
2. A MEASUREMENT OF MASS IN THE US
3. ONE OF THE SCALES TO MEASURE TEMPERATURE
5. INSTRUMENT USED TO DETECT AND RECORD EARTHQUAKES
6. UNIT OF VOLUME IN THE METRIC SYSTEM
7. DEVICE USED TO MEASURE PRESSURE
8. DEVICE USED TO MEASURE ALTITUDE
11. UNIT OF LENGTH IN THE US

ACROSS
4. THIS INSTRUMENT DISPLAYS THE SPEED OF A VEHICLE
9. A MEASUREMENT OF MASS IN THE METRIC SYSTEM
10. A MEASUREMENT OF LENGTH IN THE METRIC SYSTEM
12. DEVICE USED FOR MEASURING WIND SPEED

THE LAST CHALLENGE...

RULES OF THE GAME

FIND A DICE AND A MARKER (IT COULD BE A PEN CAP OR A COIN, FOR EXAMPLE).

PLACE YOUR MARKERS ON THE SQUARE MARKED "**START**."

EACH PLAYER TAKES A TURN ROLLING THE DICE AND MOVING FORWARD THE NUMBER OF SPACES SHOWN ON THE DICE. YOU MUST ANSWER THE QUESTION ON THE SQUARE YOU LAND ON. IF THE ANSWER IS CORRECT, YOU CAN ROLL THE DICE WHEN IT IS YOUR TURN AGAIN. IF YOU ANSWER INCORRECTLY, YOU MUST SKIP A TURN. THE OBJECT OF THE GAME IS TO BE THE FIRST PLAYER TO REACH THE "**FINISH**" SQUARE (THE ONE WITH A VOLCANO ON IT) BY THROWING THE EXACT NUMBER ON THE DICE. OTHERWISE YOU WILL HAVE TO GO BACK THE EXCESS NUMBER OF SPACES.

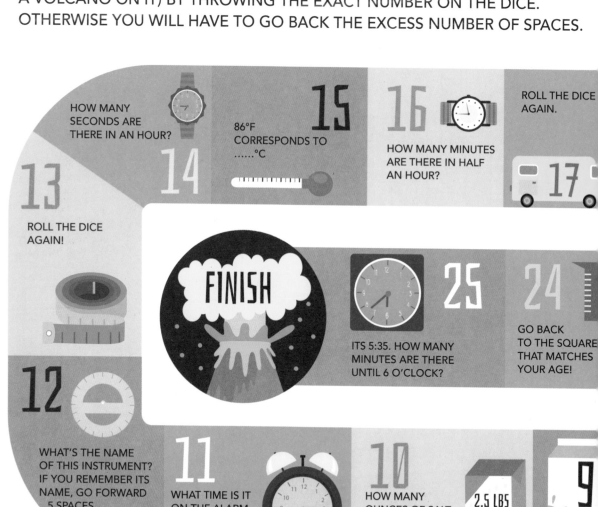

14 HOW MANY SECONDS ARE THERE IN AN HOUR?

15 86°F CORRESPONDS TO ......°C

16 HOW MANY MINUTES ARE THERE IN HALF AN HOUR?

17 ROLL THE DICE AGAIN.

13 ROLL THE DICE AGAIN!

FINISH

25 ITS 5:35. HOW MANY MINUTES ARE THERE UNTIL 6 O'CLOCK?

24 GO BACK TO THE SQUARE THAT MATCHES YOUR AGE!

12 WHAT'S THE NAME OF THIS INSTRUMENT? IF YOU REMEMBER ITS NAME, GO FORWARD 5 SPACES.

11 WHAT TIME IS IT ON THE ALARM CLOCK?

10 HOW MANY OUNCES OF SALT ARE THERE IN THIS BOX? 2.5 LBS

9

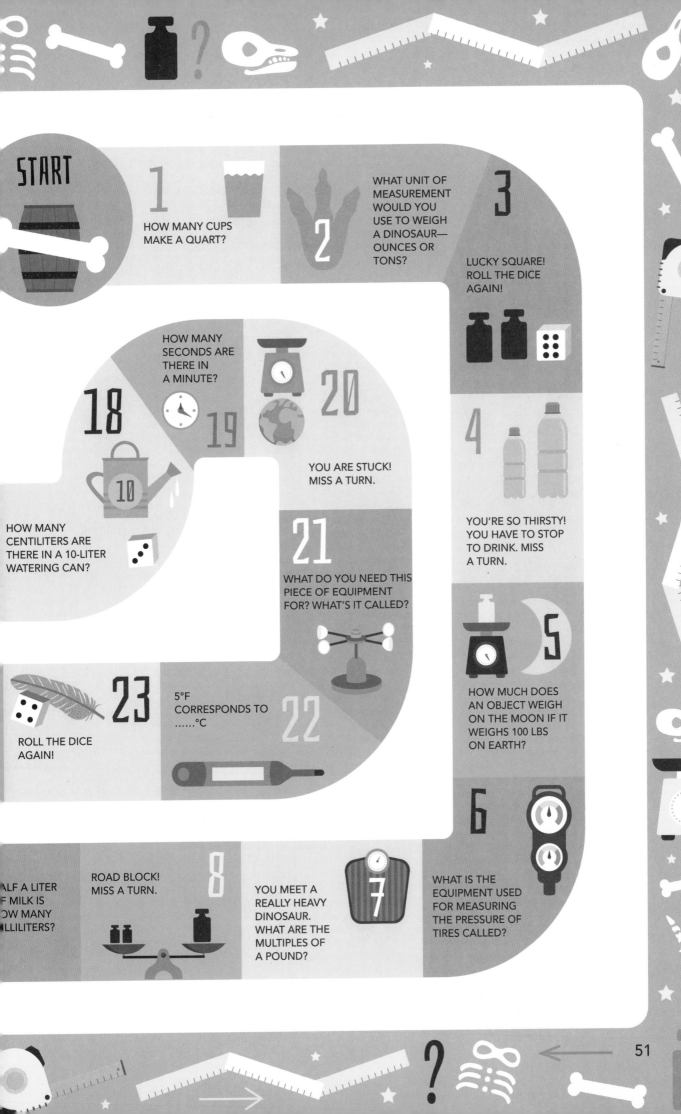

START

1 HOW MANY CUPS MAKE A QUART?

2 WHAT UNIT OF MEASUREMENT WOULD YOU USE TO WEIGH A DINOSAUR— OUNCES OR TONS?

3 LUCKY SQUARE! ROLL THE DICE AGAIN!

4 YOU'RE SO THIRSTY! YOU HAVE TO STOP TO DRINK. MISS A TURN.

5 HOW MUCH DOES AN OBJECT WEIGH ON THE MOON IF IT WEIGHS 100 LBS ON EARTH?

6 WHAT IS THE EQUIPMENT USED FOR MEASURING THE PRESSURE OF TIRES CALLED?

7 YOU MEET A REALLY HEAVY DINOSAUR. WHAT ARE THE MULTIPLES OF A POUND?

8 ROAD BLOCK! MISS A TURN.

HALF A LITER OF MILK IS HOW MANY MILLILITERS?

18 HOW MANY CENTILITERS ARE THERE IN A 10-LITER WATERING CAN?

19 HOW MANY SECONDS ARE THERE IN A MINUTE?

20 YOU ARE STUCK! MISS A TURN.

21 WHAT DO YOU NEED THIS PIECE OF EQUIPMENT FOR? WHAT'S IT CALLED?

22 5°F CORRESPONDS TO ......°C

23 ROLL THE DICE AGAIN!

51

SOLUTIONS

PP. 8–9: THE GARDEN

P. 11: MULTIPLES AND SUBDIVISIONS OF THE FOOT

3 FEET ARE A **YARD**.
A **FOOT** IS MADE UP OF 12 INCHES.
1,760 YARDS MAKE A **MILE**.

PP. 12–13: MEASUREMENTS IN THE TOWN

CAR: 5'3"
BRIDGE: 1,764 YARDS, 6 INCHES
BENCH: 44 INCHES
RIVER: JUST OVER 3,500 YARDS

A 7.5 SIZE SHOE: 9.75 INCHES
A US DOLLAR BILL: (6.2 INCHES)
A MAPLE LEAF: 4.25 INCHES
A PLASTIC SPOON: 5.5 INCHES
DIAMETER OF A BASEBALL: 9 INCHES
TOY TRAIN: 7.25 INCHES

PP. 14–15: SHOPPING IN TOWN

STEGGIE WALKS 31 FEET.
TRIXIE WALKS 576 INCHES.

PP. 18–19: THE AREAS OF THE BUILDINGS

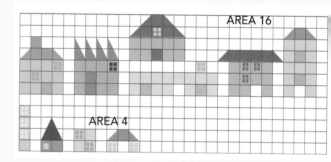

PP. 16–17: DINO'S ROUTE

DINO FOLLOWS THIS ROUTE
TO GET TO THE FAIRGROUNDS.

PP. 20–21 : BATTLESHIP

4/6/4/4
4 + 6 + 4 + 4 = 18

PP. 22–23: PENTOMINOES

THE AREA OF THE RECTANGLE MADE
UP OF 12 SHAPES = 60 SQUARES

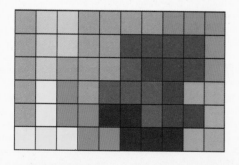

P. 24: DINOSAURS' WEIGHT

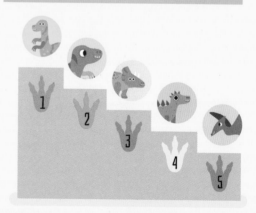

PP. 26–27: MULTIPLES AND SUBDIVISIONS OF A POUND

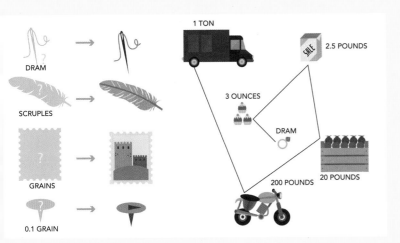

P. 28: FRUIT AND VEGETABLE BASKETS

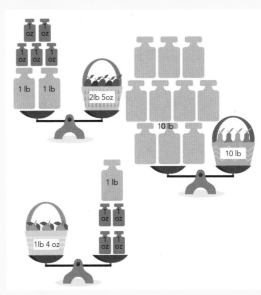

P. 29: THE CAKE

SUGAR: 64 GRAMS
BUTTER: 32 GRAMS
2 EGGS
VANILLA EXTRACT: 8 GRAMS
FLOUR: 96 GRAMS
BAKING POWDER: 6 GRAMS
MILK: 32 GRAMS

HOW WAS THE CAKE?

PP. 32–33: CUPS, PINTS, QUARTS AND GALLONS

6 1/2 - 4 1/2 - 1 3/4

PP. 30–31: HIDDEN CUPS

P. 34: HOURS, MINUTES, AND SECONDS

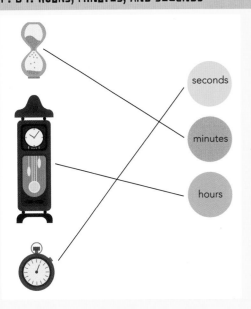

P. 36: CLOCKS

10:00   2:37   7:15

6:35   3:52   8:51

4:23   12:47   10:02

P. 37: DIGITAL CLOCKS

- 8:00
- 3:00
- 5:15
- 10:30

PP. 38–39: HOW MUCH TIME HAS PASSED?

TIME: 9:10
25 MINUTES HAVE PASSED SINCE 8:45.
TIME: 3:40
10 MINUTES HAVE PASSED SINCE 3:30.
TIME: 6:45
90 MINUTES HAVE PASSED SINCE 5:15.

IT'S 5:00 O'CLOCK; AFTER 15 MINUTES, IT'S 5:15.

IT'S 3:00 O'CLOCK; AFTER 9 HOURS IT'S 12 O'CLOC
OR MIDNIGHT.

IT'S 2:00 O'CLOCK; AFTER 45 MINUTES IT'S 2:45.

P. 40: THERMOMETERS

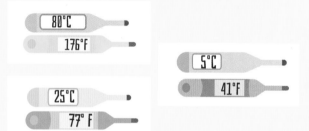

80°C
176°F

5°C
41°F

25°C
77°F

P. 41: DEGREES °C AND DEGREES °F

WATER BOILS AT: 212°F OR 100°C
OUTSIDE THE WINDOW: 86°F OR 30°C
FRIDGE: 41°F OR 5°C
FREEZER: - 20°F OR -20°C
CUP OF TEA: 122°F OR 50°C
HOT OVEN: 365°F OR 180°C

PP. 42–43: THE DINOLYMPICS

5,527 INCHES

123 SECONDS

P. 44: WEIGHTLIFTING

1ST PLACE: BRONTO
203 DRAMS/16 = 12.69 OZ
4352 OZ + 12.69 OZ = 4,364.69 OZ
4364.69/16 = 272.79 LBS
272.79 LBS + 31 LBS = 303.39 LBS
2ND PLACE: STEGGIE
864 OZ/16 = 54 LBS
54 LBS + 55 LBS = 109 LBS
3RD PLACE: DINO
700 DRAMS/16 = 43.75 OZ
43.75 OZ /16 = 2.73 LBS
77 LBS + 2.73 LBS = 79.73 LBS

P. 45: EQUIPMENT AND MEASUREMENTS

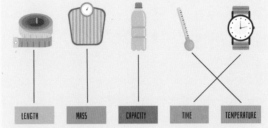

P. 46: THE ODD ONES OUT

HERE ARE **THE ODD ONES OUT**:
DINO: CUBIT
STEGGIE: MILES
TERRI: POUND
TRIXIE: FEET
BRONTO: INCHES

P. 47: DOMINOES

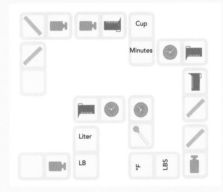

P.49: CROSSWORD

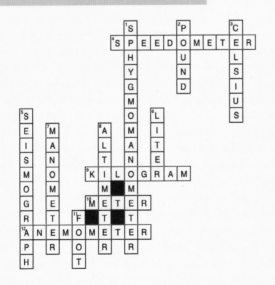

PP. 50–51: BOARD GAME

SQUARE 1: 4 CUPS = 1 QUART
SQUARE 2: TONS
SQUARE 5: AN OBJECT THAT WEIGHS 100 LBS ON EARTH WEIGHS 16.6 LBS ON THE MOON
SQUARE 6: MANOMETER
SQUARE 7: A HUNDREDWEIGHT AND A TON
SQUARE 9: HALF A LITER = 500 ML
SQUARE 10: 2.5 LBS = 40 OZ
SQUARE 11: IT'S 8:15
SQUARE 12: A PROTRACTOR MEASURES ANGLES
SQUARE 14: THERE ARE 3,600 SECONDS IN AN HOUR
SQUARE 15: 30°C = 86°F
SQUARE 16: THERE ARE 30 MINUTES IN HALF AN HOUR
SQUARE 18: 10 LITERS = 1,000 CL
SQUARE 19: THERE ARE 60 SECONDS IN A MINUTE
SQUARE 21: THE ANEMOMETER MEASURES THE WIND
SQUARE 22: 5°F = -15°C
SQUARE 25: AT 5:35 THERE ARE 25 MINUTES UNTIL 6:00

MATTIA CRIVELLINI

Mattia has a degree in computer science from the University of Bologna in Italy and studied cognitive sciences at Indiana University in the United States. Since 2011, he has been the director of Fosforo, the science festival in Senigallia, Italy. He organizes and plans activities, conferences, and shows for the communication and dissemination of science in Italy and abroad, through the NEXT Cultural Association.

VALERIA BARATTINI

Valeria holds a master's degree in economics and management of arts and cultural activities from the University of Ca 'Foscari in Venice and a master's in standards for museum education from the Roma Tre University in Rome. She works in education and cultural planning. Since 2015, she has been working in partnership with Fosforo, organizing events and activities related to the dissemination of science and informal teaching.

AGNESE BARUZZI

Agnese has a degree in graphic design from ISIA (Institute of Higher Education in the Artistic Industries) in Urbino, Italy. Since 2001, she has been working as an illustrator and author. She has produced numerous children's books in Italy and abroad. She holds workshops for children and adults, collaborating with schools and libraries. In recent years, she has beautifully illustrated several books for White Star Kids.

WHITE STAR KIDS

White Star Kids® is a registered trademark property of White Star s.r.l.

© 2021 White Star s.r.l.
Piazzale Luigi Cadorna, 6
20123 Milan, Italy
www.whitestar.it

Translation: TperTradurre S.r.l., Rome
Editing: Michele Suchomel-Casey

ISBN 978-88-544-1747-2
1 2 3 4 5 6   25 24 23 22 21

Printed in China

— 0
— 1
— 2
— 3
— 4
— 5
— 6
— 7
— 8
— 9
— 10
— 11
— 12

— 12
— 13
— 14
— 15
— 16
— 17
— 18
— 19
— 20
— 21
— 22
— 23
— 24

— 24
— 25
— 26
— 27
— 28
— 29
— 30
— 31
— 32
— 33
— 34
— 35
— 36

— 36
— 37
— 38
— 39
— 40
— 41
— 42
— 43
— 44
— 45
— 46
— 47
— 48

— 48
— 49
— 50
— 51
— 52
— 53
— 54
— 55
— 56
— 57
— 58
— 59
— 60

PAGE 24: WHO WEIGHS THE MOST?

PAGE 26: WEIGHING LIGHTER OBJECTS

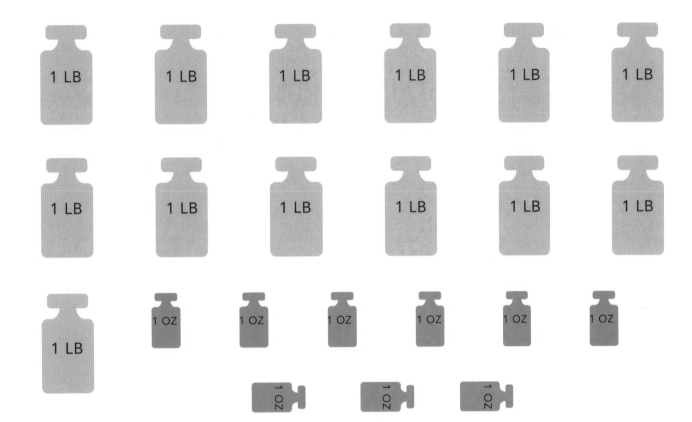

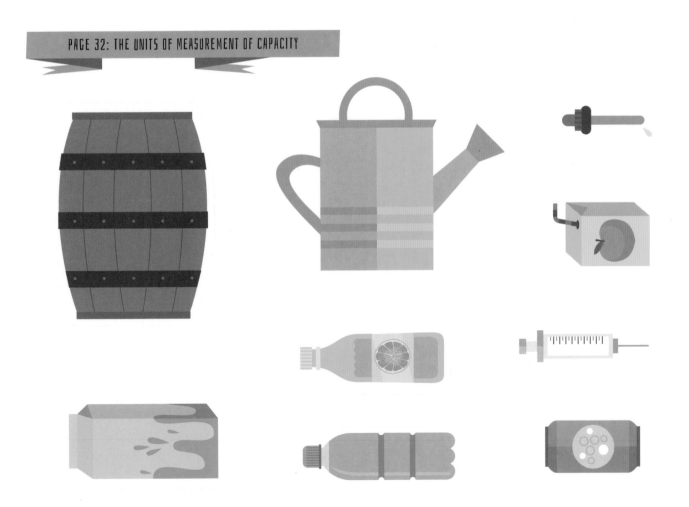

8:00

9:10

5:15

6:15

11:05

10:30

3:00

7:45

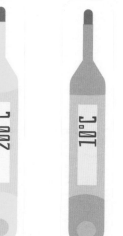

80°C

77°C

200°C

10°C

5°C

90°C

PAGE 44: THE WEIGHTLIFTING COMPETITION

PAGE 45: TOOLS AND MEASURES

PAGE 47: THE DOMINOES OF MEASUREMENTS

Cup

Minutes

°F | LBS

°C | Gallon

Liter

LB

Foot | Hour

Pound | Pint

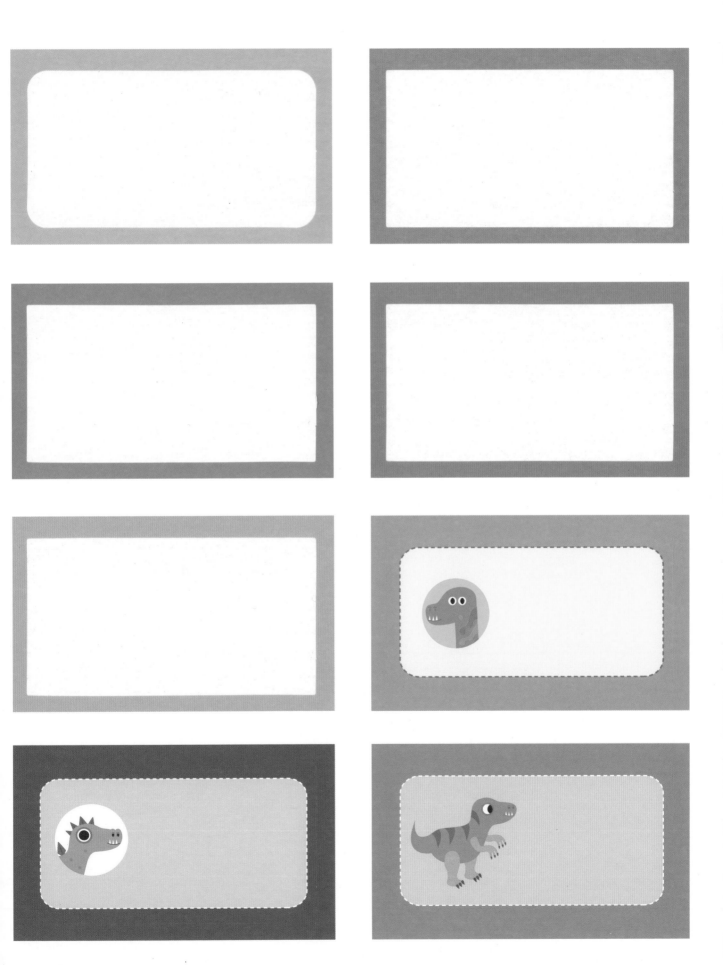

PERSONALIZE YOUR NOTEBOOKS WITH THESE LABELS!